better together*

*This book is best read together, grownup and kid.

akidsco.com

a
kids
book
about

a kids book about SUICIDE

by Angela N. Frazier

a
kids
book
about

Printed in the United States of America.

A Kids Book About books are available online: *akidsco.com*

To share your stories, ask questions, or inquire about bulk purchases (schools, libraries, and nonprofits), please use the following email address: *hello@akidsco.com*

ISBN: 978-1-951253-71-4

Designed by Rick DeLucco
Edited by Denise Morales Soto

To my mom and dad
for always reminding me
that I was unstoppable.

To my grandma, aunts, and uncles
for always believing in me enough to
invest in my dreams. But most importantly,
to the kiddo reading this book—
you are unstoppable too.

Intro

I know suicide is a tough topic to discuss with anyone. Talking about it with a kid can be especially intimidating, so I commend you for tackling this subject. As you move forward, keep in mind that kids know more than we realize. It's likely this is not the first time they have heard the word suicide. Kids are fearless in many ways; oftentimes we are the ones holding on to fear, which is understandable.

I hope this book helps you start an open conversation about suicide with your kid, answer their questions, and honor their feelings. The best part is—you will be there every step of the way. You've got this!

SUICIDE is a subject you probably won't hear much about in school or even at home.

Grownups are usually too nervous to talk about it because they think it's too scary, uncomfortable, or heavy to bring up...

especially to kids.

But maybe you are ready to talk about it.

What do you think?*

*Remember, even if something is new or uncomfortable, it doesn't mean you can't handle it.

If you do feel like you're ready, then turn to the next page. »

My name is ANGELA
and I want to talk to you
about suicide.

**Suicide is when someone dies
by taking their own life.**

It's not something that happened to
them or that someone did to them.

They did it to themselves.

**When someone dies,
usually, you can point to a reason...**

like a serious car accident,

or a life-threatening illness,

or old age.

But death is more complicated
when it comes to suicide,
which makes it really hard
to understand and talk about.

When someone you know dies by suicide you might feel...

CONFUSED, MAD, SAD, OR EVEN LONELY.

Have you ever known someone who died by suicide?

How did it make you feel?

Along with all of those
feelings, suicide can lead
to a lot of questions.

WHY DID THEY DO IT?

HOW DID IT HAPPEN?

WILL I EVER SEE THEM AGAIN?

WHY DID THEY LEAVE ME?

DID THEY NOT LOVE ME ANYMORE?

I want you to know
that all of these questions are

NOR

MAL.

I asked them myself.

Let me tell you my story.

Tami Best was my best friend...

she is also my mother.

She loved
Costco chocolate cake,
her sister's macaroni and cheese,
listening to music,
and was always the most
stunning person in the room.

I remember her smile the most.

It was big and bright and she always had it on. She would smile when she was happy and even when she was sad.

She also had severe depression.

That's when someone
isn't just sad sometimes
but feels like sadness has
taken over their entire life.

This can cause them to
sleep all day but still feel tired,
eat too much or not enough,
have trouble focusing,
and even lose interest in
activities they'd normally enjoy.

And it meant she
didn't want to go to the park,
attend my track meets,
make dinner for the family,
or even get out of bed
some days.

On her good days,
we still watched movies,
celebrated birthdays,
and had a lot of fun together.

But as time passed,
those good days became
harder to come by.

She died by suicide
when I was 24 years old.

**At first, I was shocked.
I didn't know how to feel.**

I was confused.

Then I felt sad.

Then I felt really mad.

I felt like I was disposable.*

*Disposable means to feel like you've been
thrown away or forgotten about.

Because she was gone, my mom wouldn't get to see me going off to college, would miss out on my wedding day, and wouldn't get to meet her grandchildren.

I just kept thinking about
all the things that *she* would miss
and how much I missed *her*,
but over time I realized that
I couldn't let that sadness
get the best of me.

Each of these big milestones
would still be wonderful
and worth celebrating.

How am I doing now?

Well, some days I'm OK.

Other days, I'm not OK.

There are times
when I feel really sad
all over again and
can't shake it off.

Some moments...

I'm relieved my mom
isn't in pain anymore.

Though I still miss her terribly.

I wish she understood
how much she'd be missed.

When someone dies by suicide, you'll often hear people say things like..

THEY'RE SELFISH.

YOU SHOULD HAVE
DONE SOMETHING.

HOW DID YOU NOT KNOW
SOMETHING WAS WRONG?

Or they might say things to try to help and make you feel better, like...

Everything is going to be OK.

Time heals all wounds.

They're in a better place.

But while all of these
come from a good place,
they can still hurt your feelings
or cause you more pain.

I want you to know that
no matter what you're feeling
or what people say...

IT'S NOT YOUR FAULT.

IT'S OK TO FEEL SAD.

Even if it gets better with time,
it's OK to recognize
that things are bad right now.

**You have permission
to feel however you feel.**

These emotions may come and go at different times in your life.

You might feel better for a while then feel sad all over again 1, 2, or even 10 years later.

THAT'S NORMAL TOO.

If you're a kid who has lost someone to suicide...

YOU'RE NOT ALONE.

YOU DID NOTHING WRONG.

THEY WERE IN A LOT OF PAIN.

AND THERE'S NOTHING YOU COULD
HAVE SAID OR DONE DIFFERENTLY.

If you're a kid who struggles
with thoughts of suicide...

YOU'RE NOT ALONE.

I've felt that way before too.
And I want you to know that...

YOUR LIFE IS WORTH LIVING.

YOU WOULD BE GREATLY MISSED.

YOU'RE HERE FOR A REASON.

Before you close this book, I want you to know that it is important to talk to a grownup if you are having thoughts of suicide or thoughts you don't understand.

YOU CAN TALK TO:

TEACHERS

FAMILY

PRINCIPALS

COACHES

CLERGY:
YOUR PASTOR,
PRIEST, PREACHER,
RABBI, IMAM

DOCTORS

And if you or someone you know is suffering from suicidal thoughts and live in the United States of America, please call

1-800-273-8255 to reach the **National Suicide Prevention Lifeline.**

THEY'RE HERE TO HELP.

Outro

You did it! Suicide can be complicated to navigate but I'm glad you took this opportunity to open up about it with the kids in your life. It's common at this moment to wonder what the next steps look like. First, I would recommend doing a temperature check and see how they feel after reading this book. What emotions are they feeling? Remind them that anything they might be feeling is valid. Remind them that they are here for a reason and have a purpose in this life. Most importantly, remind them that they are not alone. As you are encouraging your kiddo, know I am rooting for you too! We are all in this together.

notes

notes

kids
book
about
GOD

by Paul J. Pastor

kids
book
about
PUBLIC)))
SPEAKING

by TEDxPortland

kids
book
about
alzheimer's

by Tanya Iovino & Kiki Kouris

kids
book
about
creativity

by Sara & Stewart Scott-Curran

a
kids
book
about
CHANGE

by David Kim

a
kids
book
about
DESIGN

by Jason Mayden

a
kids
book
about
failyure

by Dr. Laymon Hicks

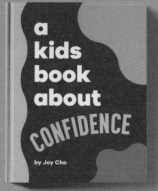

a
kids
book
about
CONFIDENCE

by Joy Cho

a
kids
book
about
IDENTITY

by Taboo

a
kids
book
about
AUTISM

by Justin P. Flood & David Flood

a
kids
book
about
COMMUNITY

by Shane Feldman

a
kids
book
about
systemic
racism

by Jordan Thierry

a
kids
book
about
grief

by Brennan C. Wood
in partnership with Dougy Center

a
kids
book
about

by Nakita Simpson
a coloring book experience

a
kids
book
about
FEMINISM

by Emma Mcilroy

a
kids
book
about
belonging

by Kevin Carroll
Bestselling Author of
Rules of the Red Rubber Ball

ds
k
out

a
kids
book
about
adventure

a
kids
book
about
white
privilege

a
kids
book
about
Sexual

a
kids
book
about

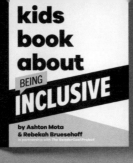

a kids book about BEING INCLUSIVE
by Ashton Mota & Rebekah Bruesehoff
in partnership with The GenderCool Project

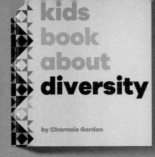

kids book about diversity
by Charnaie Gordon

kids book about LEADErSHIP
by Orion Jean

kids book about IMMIGRA

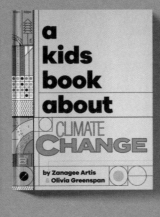

a kids book about CLIMATE CHANGE
by Zanagee Artis & Olivia Greenspan

a kids book about IMAGINATION
by LEVAR BURTON

a kids book about GENDER
by Dale Mueller

a kids book abo Sex Ab
by Evelyn Yan

a kids book about YOUR MICROBIOME
by Ara Katz
in partnership with Seed

a kids book about racism
by Jelani Memory

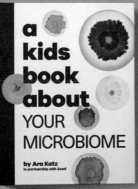

a kids book about DISABILITIES
by Kristine Napper

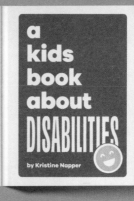

a kids book about bored
by: KYLE STEED

a kids book about cancer
by Dr. Kelsie Storm & Sarah Porter

a kids book about BEING TRANSGENDER
by Gia Parr
in partnership with The GenderCool Project

a kids book about DEPRESSION
by Kileah McIlvain

a kid boo abo ptin
by Meir Kay

a kids book about THE TULSA

Visit us at akidsco.com to discover more stories.

EXPLORE MORE IN OUR APP.

Scan the QR code
to download today!